Artificial Intelligence for Environmental Conservation

Tackling Climate Change

Table of Contents

Chapter 1. Introduction

In this special report, we delve into the fascinating intersection of advanced tech and environmental activism: "Artificial Intelligence for Environmental Conservation: Tackling Climate Change". Guiding you through both unfamiliar terrains and exciting opportunities, this report makes the complex science of AI accessible and engaging. Uncovering how AI, far beyond its popular use in self-driving cars or voice recognition software, is becoming an indispensable tool in the fight against climate change, we spotlight ingenious AI applications that simplify elusive climatic data and provide actionable solutions. From predicting weather patterns to monitoring ecosystem health and carbon tracking, this report will illuminate how AI in environmental conservation is not just about the future but is making a tangible difference right here, right now. Ready to embark on this invigorating journey and grasp the full potential of this powerful alliance of tech and conservation? Your voyage into a more sustainable and AI-driven world starts here.

Chapter 2. Unveiling Artificial Intelligence: Defying the Mystique

As we approach the union of frontier technology and environmental conservation, the inherent mystique of Artificial Intelligence (AI) merits extensive demystification. It is possible, after all, that some of the purpose and intuitiveness behind AI remains obscure amidst the flurry of its popular applications.

To realize the transformational potential of AI in combating climate change, it is important for us to first understand its basic definition, its operational layers and the dynamics of its function. Our journey through this exploratory chapter starts with defining the elusive AI.

2.1. What is Artificial Intelligence?

At the most fundamental level, AI refers to the simulation of human intelligence in machines, specifically computer systems. It is a branch of computer science that aims to create systems able to perform tasks that would require human intelligence, such as learning, reasoning, problem-solving, perception, and language understanding.

In the broad spectrum of AI, two categories emerge: Narrow AI and General AI. Narrow AI, often known as "weak AI", is a system designed and trained for a specific task — such as voice recognition, recommendation systems or image recognition — which are often seen in the tools, apps and devices we use today. On the other hand, General AI, often known as "strong AI", is systems or devices that can understand, learn, adapt and implement knowledge across a wide array of tasks, showing levels of cognitive capability comparable to a human being. Though the concept of General AI is the subject of much speculative fiction and future-gazing, it is currently confined to the realm of theory and research.

2.2. The Layers of AI: Machine Learning and Deep Learning

The operational process of AI is not confined to a singular, monolithic structure. Rather, it organizes itself into layers, or sub-fields, that work together to create the full AI experience. The primary layers include Machine Learning (ML) and Deep Learning.

Machine Learning is a method of data analysis that automates analytical model building. It is a branch of artificial intelligence based on the concept that systems can learn from data, identify patterns and make decisions with minimal human intervention.

Within Machine Learning, there's a more specific sub-layer called Deep Learning. Deep Learning, a subset of Machine Learning, employs artificial neural networks with several layers - or "depth" - thereby enabling the machine to learn and make intelligent decisions on its own.

2.3. How AI Works: An Overview

AI functions predominantly through a combination of extensive data input and complex algorithms. Simply put, an algorithm in this context is a set of statistical processing steps. The AI system is 'trained' using large data sets, where the algorithm learns the patterns and rules, and then applies them for future predictions.

Data quantity plays a crucial role in the effectiveness of AI. The more data available for training, the more accurately AI can make predictions, identify patterns and perform tasks. Without sufficient data, an AI system may struggle to find relevancy or develop any useful predictive capabilities.

2.4. The Power of AI: Potential and Pitfalls

AI represents a potent force for change, bridging the gap between complexity and usability in many domains. Specifically, in an environmental context, AI can perform tasks such as analyzing vast amounts of climatic data or predicting weather patterns with a speed and accuracy that far exceeds human capabilities. It can also enable real-time monitoring and decision-making in critical situations.

Despite this potential, the development and use of AI are not without their pitfalls. Concerns ranging from data privacy, potential job displacement, and the ethical complexities surrounding AI decision-making are prevalent. AI systems can also mirror and amplify existing biases present in the data they're fed, leading to issues of fairness and transparency. It's our responsibility to navigate these concerns with care as we harness the full potential of AI.

2.5. AI in Context: Climate Change and Environmental Conservation

While AI's popular uses in technology and lifestyle applications are well-known, its potential role in environmental conservation and climate change is still being discovered. By demystifying AI, we can begin to see the potential of this powerful tool in tackling these global challenges. The complex algorithms, extensive data analysis capabilities, and predictive modelling potential of AI could shed light on the elusive enigma of climate change and provide us with practical, actionable solutions.

Reflecting on the facets of AI we've unveiled, we proceed to the next chapter, where we delve into how AI can specifically be applied to environmental conservation and climate change mitigation. The underlying power of AI to analyze, predict, and provide data-driven solutions will be key to unlocking unprecedented opportunities in our fight against global warming and the pursuit of a sustainable future.

Chapter 3. From Silicon Valleys to Green Fields: The AI Transition

Technology is driving a profound transformation from Silicon Valleys to green fields, harnessing artificial intelligence (AI) to tackle critical environmental issues and catapult our transition towards a sustainable future.

3.1. The Era of Tech-Driven Environmental Conservation

The heartland of tech innovation, Silicon Valley, is known for birthing digital giants like Facebook, Google, and Apple. However, in recent years, a new breed of startups has emerged, whose ambitious aspiration is not only about pioneering technology but also about mobilizing it for the benefit of our environment. Amidst this outstanding fusion, AI sits at the core, creating a framework that enables data interpretation and pattern recognition on an unprecedented scale for environmental conservation.

AI platforms, developed by both emerging startups and tech giants alike, are generating real-time analytics to predict, monitor, and respond to environmental changes. They are facilitating evidence-based decision-making by collecting, analyzing, and interpreting vast amounts of environmental data, transforming the way we approach climate change and environmental conservation.

These applications range from identifying illegal logging using satellite footage to predicting drought patterns and their impact on food production, thereby guiding policy and decision-making. They set a significant precedent, reinforcing the role of technology as a conduit for positive change, and establishing AI's potential in shaping a sustainable future.

3.2. Data Collection, Monitoring, and Analysis

One of the critical contributions of AI in this regard is its capability to process voluminous environmental data. This data ranges from local weather station information, global climatic data, wildlife migratory patterns, oceanographic data, to satellite imagery. AI algorithms and deep learning models are designed to extract meaningful insights from these datasets, fostering a predictive, preemptive, rather than reactionary approach to environmental conservation policies.

For instance, monitoring forest cover across large swathes of land through manual means is both strenuous and time-consuming. Yet, AI can evaluate chunks of satellite imagery to detect deforestation activities, enhancing our capacity to prevent detrimental actions that contribute towards climate change.

Similarly, AI-driven models have been developed to monitor the health of coral reefs, a critical component of our ocean ecosystems. By analyzing thousands of images using machine learning, these models identify changes, helping biologists and conservationists take immediate action. The confluence of technology and environment indicates how Silicon Valley's digital innovation is finding resonance in the green fields.

3.3. Predictive Analytics and Environmental Modelling

Equally transformative is the application of AI in generating predictive models for environmental phenomena. AI algorithms can sift through historical weather and climatic data and discern patterns that can help predict future trends.

For instance, startups are deploying AI models to predict weather patterns and facilitate farmers' decision-making in the context of planting and harvesting crops. Other AI-driven tools can predict the influx of pests, equipping farmers with proactive measures to tackle them without excessive dependence on chemical pesticides.

AI can also help in understanding climate change at macro levels. Machine learning algorithms can link trends across different datasets, such as carbon emissions, deforestation rates, and global temperatures, correlating them to assess future climate scenarios. By modelling such potential futures, AI tools can support policymakers in setting priorities and formulating climate interventions.

3.4. AI and Renewable Energy

AI finds a significant application in renewable energy, from optimizing energy generation to predicting demand and managing distribution networks. It can analyze historical data, weather forecasts, and real-time energy production from wind and solar farms, and utilize this data to manage the energy grid efficiently - not only improving energy production but reducing wastage as well.

AI can also assist in creating 'smart grids', integrating diverse energy sources and managing energy output according to demand effectively. Furthermore, it can forecast solar and wind energy output, thereby ensuring reliable power supply while reducing dependence on non-renewable sources.

Certainly, this represents just the tip of the iceberg, and we are bound to witness an increasing proliferation of AI in managing our transition to green, renewable energy sources.

In conclusion, the notion of Silicon Valleys morphing into green fields - where technology enhances environmental conservation rather than contributes to its degradation – is not beyond reach. The innovative applications of AI envision a new era of environmental conservation, aided by technology, and bring into focus the interoperability between human invention and nature. Through AI, we are not only expanding the horizons of what is technically feasible but also redefining what is environmentally desirable, inciting a meaningful dialogue between the realms of technological innovation and ecological preservation.

Chapter 4. Climate Change: The Challenges and Effects

Understanding climate change's increasingly severe manifestations is integral to comprehensive action plans. In the quest for sustainable future, humanity grapples with numerous challenges but also wields promising tools to combat their effects.

4.1. Climate Change: An Overview

At its core, climate change represents long-term shifts in average weather patterns. While some consider it a new phenomenon, Earth has experienced periods of climatic change throughout history. However, the present period of warming is distinctive. Scientists attribute the cause to an upsurge in greenhouse gases primarily due to human activities like deforestation, industrialization, and combustion of fossil fuels.

The Earth's atmosphere is a complex system, interacting dynamically with other elements in the planetary ecosystem, shaping our environment. An increase in the concentration of greenhouse gases tips this balance, trapping more heat from the Sun, leading to a 'greenhouse effect.' This rise in the Earth's average temperature is known as global warming - a primary compounding factor of climatic change.

4.2. The Adverse Effects of Climate Change

The impacts of climate change are far-reaching and manifest in various forms. These effects invariably signal an upset in Earth's systems, crucially affecting both human lives and biodiversity.

4.2.1. Rising Sea Levels

One of the most palpable impacts of global warming is the rising sea levels. Warmer temperatures cause polar ice to melt, contributing to the expansion of ocean water, both processes increasing the volume of water in the seas. This phenomenon threatens to flood coastal cities, many of which are densely populated, and submerge low-lying islands.

4.2.2. Increased Intensity of Weather Events

Global warming ignites more vigorous and frequent extreme weather events, such as hurricanes, heatwaves, and heavy precipitation. These incidents result in catastrophic loss of lives, property, and ecosystems; further, they strain resources and infrastructure with their recovery requirements.

4.2.3. Altered Ecological Systems

Climate change alters the delicate balance of ecosystems. A slight shift in temperature can transform habitats, affecting the flora and fauna that depend on these conditions for survival. Changes in migration patterns, seasonal changes, and disruptions in food chains are often witnessed. Endangered populations and the increased rate of species extinction present one of the gravest effects of climate change.

4.2.4. Human Health Risks

Climate change also poses significant risks to human health. Increased heatwaves can lead to heat stroke and dehydration. Changes in weather patterns may lead to spread of infectious diseases as vectors can inhabit new regions. Moreover, extreme weather events contribute to mental health stressors and nutrition scarcity, due to disrupted food production.

4.3. Climate Change Challenges: The Effort to Mitigate

Morally compelled to act, and with scientific consensus advising urgent measures, mankind faces many challenges in mitigating climate change effects.

4.3.1. Lowering Greenhouse Gas Emissions

Reducing greenhouse gases, especially carbon dioxide, is arguably the most critical task. This would involve reimagining economic systems to deviate from the greenhouse-gas-intensive energy sources we currently rely on. It requires advancements in technology, changes to industrial processes, and overhaul of transportation and agricultural methods.

4.3.2. Climate Change Adaptation

Simultaneously, efforts are required to build a world that can more effectively withstand the impacts of climate changes that are already inevitable. This implies engineering more resilient infrastructures, developing efficient emergency services, and safeguarding public health.

4.3.3. International Cooperation

Climate change is a global problem, transcending international borders. It calls for worldwide coordination and cooperation on emission reductions, wealth transfer to support developing countries' adaptation, and collective research efforts. The challenge lies in negotiating the diverse interests and capabilities of different nations.

4.4. The Auxiliary Role of Advanced Technologies

Advanced technologies, such as AI, can play a transformative role in combating climate change. However, they are not the magic bullet solutions. While they can greatly augment human efforts, they cannot indefinitely overcome the physical limitations posed by the laws of nature.

Climate change presents us with an immediate, multifaceted problem that requires equally comprehensive solutions. Emerging technologies, harnessed properly and promptly, can be vital aides in this monumental effort. The evolving realm of Artificial Intelligence holds the potential to revolutionize the methods of conservation, providing unexplored avenues for mitigation and a renewed hope for a sustainable future.

Chapter 5. Decoding Complexities: AI in Climate Modelling and Prediction

Modern climate prediction models leverage several techniques from the realm of artificial intelligence, including machine learning, neural networks, and more. These technologies hold the potential to infuse the domain of climatology with newfound accuracy and efficacy, driving our collective endeavour to combat climate change forward.

5.1. Machine Learning in Climatology

Machine learning, a subset of AI, thrives on identifying patterns within large and complex data sets. Weather patterns, oscillations, and aberrations are no exception. Churning through countless meteorological data points, machine learning algorithms offer accurate predictions such as potential weather patterns or the likelihood of extreme weather events.

For instance, in weather forecasting, traditional numerical models may fail to predict the possibility of rapid weather changes due to the high computational cost. Machine learning, especially the Deep Learning models, however, can discern patterns from vast historical weather data to provide accurate forecasts in real-time. NASA, for example, uses Deep Learning powered weather models to predict solar activities which can adversely affect technological systems on Earth.

Beyond just short term weather predictions, machine learning also aids in long term climate change modelling. Incorporating environmental variables including greenhouse gas emissions, atmospheric particulate matter, and land use, machine learning provides simulations of potential future climates. This meaningful contribution of machine learning can guide policy makers in implementing efficient climate adaptation and mitigation strategies.

5.2. AI-assisted Climate Modelling Optimization

While climate models are an essential tool of climatology, the key challenge lies in their complexity and the resultant computational cost. Performance optimization of climate models is a significant area where AI is making an impact.

Ensemble modelling has been a popular technique used to reduce uncertainties in climate modelling. However, generating and analyzing an ensemble of high-resolution climate simulations is still computationally intensive. Neural networks, another AI-based technology, can help solve this problem. Researchers train these networks using a small set of high-resolution models. Once trained, the networks can generate new ensembles quickly and accurately, reducing computational effort.

In addition, AI has also been instrumental in refining parameterization within climate models. Traditional methods approximate the effects of smaller-scale processes, such as cloud formation or ocean eddies, which can lead to errors. AI-driven algorithms can learn from high-resolution simulations and actual observations, providing a more accurate parameterization and thus enhancing the robustness of the climate models.

5.3. AI in Natural Disaster Predictions and Alerts

The predictive capacity of AI goes beyond weather patterns and climate models. It is also playing a pivotal role in predicting the likelihood of natural disasters such as wildfires, cyclones, and floods, and issuing early warning alerts.

Deep learning models, processing remotely sensed data from satellites, significantly improve the accuracy in predicting the onset and course of wildfires. Predictions are vital for fire suppression strategies and in deciding the evacuation of endangered areas.

Regarding floods, machine learning algorithms analyze rainfall data and hydrologic models to predict the areas and timing of flooding. These predictions directly aid in disaster risk reduction by improving information available to emergency services and affected communities.

In the context of storm and cyclone predictions, AI based models provide a more efficient way to process large volumes of data collected from satellite images and sensors, helping forecasters track the path and intensity of storms well in advance.

5.4. Role of AI in Carbon Budgeting and Tracking

AI and machine learning provide innovative means for tracking terrestrial and atmospheric carbon levels, which are critical inputs for climate models. Satellite imagery combined with machine learning algorithms can track and predict changes in land cover, forest areas, and crop types – all of which influence the carbon cycle. They can even assess the amount of CO_2 absorbed by oceans.

Additionally, AI enables better estimating and monitoring of greenhouse gas emissions from industrial sources. Techniques like anomaly detection can help to identify sudden increases in industries' carbon outputs, thus holding them accountable for their emissions.

5.5. Future Directions of AI in Climate Predictions

Just as climate science continues to evolve, so does the role of AI within it. AI holds promise for further enhancing climate models' resolution and accuracy. For instance, harnessing Quantum Machine Learning for climate modelling and predictions could unlock new levels of accuracy, given its capitalization on quantum phenomena and exceptionally high computational powers.

AI is not without its drawbacks, however. Biases can emerge from the way data is collected and processed, which could affect model outcomes. It's crucial to continually refine the AI models, maintain transparency in methodologies, and critically evaluate results.

Indeed, AI is presenting an exciting new paradigm in climate science and environmental conservation. As this chapter has outlined, the potential for AI in climate modelling and prediction is vast and varied. From enhancing climate models to predicting natural disasters and tracking carbon levels, AI is proving to be an indispensable ally in understanding and combating climate change, leading us towards a resilient and sustainable future.

Chapter 6. The AI Watchdog: Monitoring and Tracking Climate Change

Climate change is an undeniable reality of our time, and combatting it is one of the greatest challenges we face as a planet. It is through the insights harnessed from complex patterns inherent in environmental data, that we can begin to devise tactical strategies against the multifaceted enemy of climate change. The emergence of AI, with its sophisticated predictive capabilities, might just be the game-changer we need. Monitoring and tracking climate change with AI is quickly gaining popularity as an effective tool to make sense of the complexities of climate change, all while providing actionable insights.

6.1. AI for Climate Data Analysis and Prediction

From tracking atmospheric conditions to following marine and terrestrial ecosystems' health, AI's big data utilization is proving ground-breaking in providing key insights. Vast amounts of Earth system data are available from sources such as satellites, weather stations, and ocean buoys. These data points, collectively known as 'Big Earth Data', encapsulate enormous amounts of information about our planet's climate patterns, ecosystems, and atmospheric conditions.

Traditional methodologies for examining and predicting climate conditions often fall short due to the sheer volume and complexity of data. In contrast, AI algorithms, specifically Machine Learning (ML) models are exceptionally good at finding relationships within colossal amounts of data. The power to predict weather patterns, forecast droughts, floods, and other natural disasters can be significantly improved.

6.2. AI in Surveillance for Environmental Protection

Apart from predicting environmental catastrophes, AI can significantly improve surveillance in environmental protection. For instance, deforestation and forest degradation account for approximately 15% of all greenhouse gas emissions. AI can help identify deforestation and illegal logging activities with better precision and speed. Using high-resolution satellite images, AI can spot changes that might indicate logging, forest fires, or other devastating events, providing authorities with an opportunity to act swiftly.

Similarly, AI-powered autonomous drones equipped with infrared cameras are being used for monitoring the health of wildlife and their habitats. Machine learning algorithms can identify and count wildlife individuals from aerial images captured by drones, proving much more efficient than traditional manual methods.

6.3. Tracking Greenhouse Gas Emissions with AI

Understanding and tracking carbon emissions is essential to addressing climate change. AI can assist in creating detailed carbon footprints for countries, cities, and even individual companies or households. The technology can scrutinize a vast range of data sources, such as industrial databases, auto emissions stats, building energy usage, or meter readings. Machine learning algorithms can then sort, analyze, and draw conclusions from these disparate data points, providing actionable insights for reducing carbon emissions.

An emerging application is AI's use in detecting methane leaks. Methane is a potent greenhouse gas and identifying and fixing leaks from drilling and transporting natural gas can significantly augment our fight against global warming.

6.4. AI and Ocean Health Monitoring

Oceans play a significant role in global weather patterns and effectively act as the world's largest carbon sink. Understanding the health of oceans is thus crucial. AI can help process vast quantities of data collected from sonars, satellites, and surface floats to monitor ocean temperature, pH levels, salinity, and biodiversity.

By using machine learning algorithms, we can understand changes in fish populations, find correlations with water temperatures, pH levels, and monitor plastic pollution. These analyses can help us recognize not just what is happening but why, thus enabling us to devise science-backed strategies to tackle marine pollution and global warming.

6.5. Climate Change Scenario Modelling with AI

AI also offers exceptional capabilities in climate change scenario modeling. ML algorithms can process a wide range of climate variables and their interactions over time, offering nuanced and likely future scenarios. Such models can enable us to forecast the potential impacts of climate change and the efficacy of possible mitigations.

This is of great significance as responses to climate change need not only be reactive but also proactive. Meaningfully leveraging AI can assist world leaders and policymakers in taking preemptive action against projected climate adversities.

Unraveling the complexities of climate change, and turning them into actionable insights, is perhaps one of our most powerful tactics in the fight for the planet. With its ability to analyze big data, predict outcomes, track changes, and even summon preventative measures, the AI watchdog promises not merely to observe from the sidelines of this combat but to be at the front lines, bridging the gap between understanding the momentous task at hand and taking the necessary actions. As we push against the ominous wheel of climate change, this vigilant technological giant will undoubtedly prove invaluable.

Chapter 7. Eco-warriors: AI in Wildlife Preservation and Biodiversity Conservation

As crucial as it is to curtail greenhouse gas emissions and stem the tide of global warming, saving our planet relies heavily on biodiversity conservation and the preservation of wildlife. Artificial intelligence (AI) has surged onto the scene as an indispensable ally in this endeavor. Exploiting the power of machine learning, predictive modelling, and data analysis, AI has become a game changer, helping scientists, researchers, and conservationists to monitor, protect, and restore ecosystems.

7.1. AI in Biodiversity Mapping

Biodiversity, or the complexity and variety of life on Earth, is crucial for ecosystem health. More than just a cataloging of species, biodiversity incorporates the fluctuating dynamics of life, including species' populations, their relationships with other species, and their interactions with the environment. One of the bottlenecks in biodiversity conservation has been the complexity and volume of data needed to fully understand these dynamics. AI is helping overcome this challenge through biodiversity mapping.

AI can manage, analyze, and visualize large volumes of data far more effectively and efficiently than traditional approaches. Machine learning algorithms identify patterns and correlations within the data, highlighting regions of high biodiversity and areas under threat. Leveraging high-resolution satellite imagery, AI can also track changes over time to improve conservation strategies.

7.2. AI and Species Identification

One challenging aspect of biodiversity conservation is species identification – a critical first step in any conservation strategy. Traditional methods are both time-consuming and require significant expertise. AI, using image recognition and deep learning, can automate the process and achieve significantly higher rates of accuracy.

Platforms like iNaturalist and eBird use machine learning to help amateur naturalists identify species accurately and contribute to global biodiversity databases. On a more specialized level, some AI projects are designed to identify particular species, tracking threats and enabling prompt conservation action.

7.3. Machine Learning for Monitoring Ecosystem Health

Monitoring the health of an ecosystem is no small task, particularly in vast or inaccessible areas like the Amazon rainforest or the Arctic tundra. Deploying sensor networks and utilizing satellite images, AI steps up to the task – interpreting enormous volumes of data to provide a real-time overview of the ecosystem's status.

Deep learning methods prove particularly useful here. They can analyze the forest canopy's structure to assess health, and predict future changes based on the current rate of deforestation or climate change impact. The insights generated serve as a guide for conservation initiatives, helping prioritize regions for restoration or protection.

7.4. AI in the Fight Against Poaching

The illegal wildlife trade constitutes a severe threat to biodiversity.

Implementing AI can help combat this. Systems like PAWS (Protection Assistant for Wildlife Security) use machine learning to predict poaching hotspots, enabling authorities to take preventative action.

Coupled with technologies like SMART (Spatial Monitoring and Reporting Tool), AI not just predicts poacher routes but also strategizes the best patrol routes for rangers. Drones equipped with AI image recognition can identify poachers in real-time, leading to faster response times.

7.5. Predictive Modeling for Conservation Planning

Conservation is essentially a forward-looking endeavor. Understanding future scenario probabilities based on current factors aids the formulation of effective conservation strategies.

Predictive modeling underpins this advance planning. Machine learning can process vast quantities of data to predict future trends in climate change, habitat loss, and species distribution. Such predictions create an early warning system, allowing for insightful decision-making and proactive conservation efforts.

7.6. AI and Citizen Science

Citizen science projects like the Great Backyard Bird Count and Zooniverse allow the general public to engage with conservation. AI enhances such endeavors by organizing, analyzing, and learning from the input of thousands—even millions—of volunteers.

Whether it's classifying galaxies, transcribing old ship logs, or identifying species counts in an area, AI systems work in tandem with citizen science to create vast and valuable data sets, driving powerful conservation actions.

7.7. Final Thoughts

In conclusion, AI has ushered in a new era of wildlife preservation and biodiversity conservation, enabling timely, targeted, and effective strategies. Constant advancements in AI technology promise an exciting future in ecosystem protection. Yet, the onus remains on us - policymakers, conservationists, and citizens alike - to harness the potential of AI responsibly, ensuring a sustainable coexistence with the natural world for generations to come. Development, deployment and overall digital transformation initiatives should be consistently sustainable and environment friendly. Not to mention education and awareness among masses to ensure that technological engagement is driving positive, significant change.

In essence, AI empowers us to become true eco-warriors, guiding our fight to preserve life in all its manifold, marvelous forms on this planet we call home. It's a partnership of silicon and soul that will shape the future of environmental conservation.

Chapter 8. AI and Carbon Footprinting: Pioneering Environmental Accounting

Climate change, accelerated by elevated levels of greenhouse gases (GHG) such as carbon dioxide (CO_2) in our atmosphere, presents an existential threat. Carbon accounting or footprinting – quantifying and managing CO_2 emissions – forms a crucial aspect of our response. Traditional methods offer basic insights but not the depth or speed crucial to tackling such a global threat. Enter Artificial Intelligence (AI).

AI, with its decision-making capabilities and automation technologies, brings a revolutionary change to the carbon accounting process. But how exactly does AI change the game, and what are the potential challenges and future possibilities?

8.1. AI in Carbon Footprinting: The Basics

To understand the interaction of AI and carbon footprinting, let's begin with defining these elements individually.

Carbon footprinting, in essence, evaluates the total GHG emissions caused directly or indirectly by an individual, event, organization, or product. This evaluation includes all the relevant sources of emissions related to these entities, providing a comprehensive overview of their 'carbon footprint.'

AI, contrarily, is a field of computer science focused on creating systems capable of performing tasks that usually require human intelligence. These tasks range from speech recognition and decision-making to translation between languages and visual perception.

AI's application in carbon accounting brings together the best of technology and environmental science, making the whole process more efficient, accurate, and actionable.

8.2. AI-Driven Emissions Tracking and Management

Tracking emissions at a granular level has always been challenging due to the complexity associated with data collection and analysis. AI can dramatically increase the accuracy and scope of this tracking. Machine Learning (ML), a subset of AI, is particularly beneficial in recognizing patterns and making predictions. By feeding large datasets to ML algorithms, we can accurately pinpoint the emission sources, understand their interplays, and make accurate predictions about future emissions.

Predictive analytics models, another AI-based tool, leverage past data to forecast future probabilities. This tool helps in understanding the potential effects of various activities and devising strategies accordingly. Organizations can thus plan for a more sustainable future using these AI-driven emission tracking and predictive models.

8.3. Innovations in AI and Carbon Accounting

In recent years, there have been significant innovations where AI has been used to revolutionize carbon accounting. For instance:

- Google's Environmental Insights Explorer uses AI to provide city-wide emissions data, including emissions from transportation and buildings.

- Watershed, a software platform, uses AI algorithms to calculate individual company's carbon footprints in real-time, covering direct and indirect emissions.

- Microsoft's AI for Earth initiative provides access to cloud and AI services for organizations dedicated to environmental conservation, including carbon accounting.

These show the transformative potential of AI in carbon accounting and hint at how this technology can further reimagine our efforts towards reducing global emissions.

8.4. Challenges and Limitations

While AI significantly improves carbon footprinting, several challenges remain. AI requires large datasets, but data on carbon emissions is often scattered and non-standard. Another issue is the complexity of these data. Emission metrics are affected by numerous variables, ranging from specific industrial processes to broader aspects like policy and population change.

Data privacy and security concerns present another barrier. In the wake of increasing cybersecurity threats, how to protect the data inputted into AI systems is a concern.

Despite these hurdles, the potential benefits of integrating AI within carbon footprinting far outweigh the risks.

8.5. Future Possibilities

Looking towards the future, the integration of IoT devices with AI presents a fascinating prospect. 'Smart' devices can generate and collect data on all kinds of activities, while the AI systems analyse this data to generate actionable insights into managing carbon footprints effectively.

Moreover, AI could also foster transparency by enabling the automatization and standardization of reporting carbon emissions data, thereby reducing greenwashing. Such transparency could lead to increased accountability, serving as an impetus for organizations and countries to action sustained carbon reduction plans.

The intersection of AI and environmental conservation is only just beginning to show its immense potential. AI for carbon footprinting contributes to a growing arsenal of sophisticated, digital solutions in the battle against climate change. With continued investment and research, the revolutionary application of Artificial Intelligence in carbon emission management can bring our world closer to attaining a more sustainable and balanced ecological future.

Chapter 9. Smart Agriculture: Leveraging AI for Sustainable Farming

In the vast realm of artificial intelligence applications, smart agriculture, or agriculture 4.0, emerges as a game-changing field. Deploying sophisticated tech to deliver sustainable farming practices offers complex benefits that extend beyond increasing productivity. Green agriculture protects our delicate ecosystems, reduces farming's environmental footprint, and aids in tackling the global challenge of climate change.

9.1. From Tradition to Transformation

Agriculture, an age-old practice chiefly governed by traditional knowledge and manual labor, is undergoing a remarkable transformation. As the world's population continues to burgeon, expected to reach near 10 billion by 2050, the demand for food is following suit. Meeting this ever-increasing demand while also mitigating the impact of farming on the environment is a crucial challenge. Adapting to these needs, farmers are now gradually incorporating AI-enabled tools into cultivation, harvesting, and post-harvest activities.

Modern agriculture could be barely recognizable to our ancestors, with drones, automated harvesters, and robotic milkers becoming standard equipment on large-scale farms. However, these technologies are only the beginning. AI farming solutions are transforming agriculture from being reactive to a proactive, data-driven industry.

9.2. AI Techniques Deployed in Agriculture

It's important to understand the various AI techniques currently being leveraged in agriculture.

Machine learning (ML): ML, a subset of AI, centers on the use of curated data to train algorithms, enabling them to predict outcomes without being explicitly programmed. Farmers can use ML to predict yield, understand soil health, and forecast weather conditions, among other applications.

Artificial Neural Networks (ANN): ANNs mimic the human brain's functionality, creating algorithms that can learn and improve over time. They are particularly useful in addressing non-linear problems commonly found in agriculture, such as plant diseases or pest infestations that are non-uniform in nature.

Deep learning: Deep learning, a part of ML, involves neural networks with several hidden layers. Deep learning algorithms can help identify diseases or pests in crops with accuracy that equals or even surpasses human judgment.

9.3. Predictive Analytics for Crop Management

Predictive analytics involves using statistical algorithms and machine learning techniques to identify the likelihood of future outcomes based on historical data. Farmers can employ AI tools to predict optimal planting times, select suitable crops for specific plots of land, estimate the volume of fertilizers and pesticides required, and anticipate potential risks.

These advanced algorithms also provide solutions for crop diseases and pest infestations. Farmers receive early warnings about potential threats, enabling them to take preventive measures and minimize damage.

9.4. Precision Farming

Precision farming, or precision agriculture, harnesses technology to make farming more controlled and thus more efficient. AI-driven predictive analytics, machine learning algorithms, and IoT (Internet of Things) sensors are vital tools for obtaining in-depth data about soil characteristics, crop health, and local weather conditions.

Farmers can directly send the exact quantity of water, fertilizer or pesticides required by individual plots of land, saving resources and reducing environmental impact. Moreover, precision farming enables farmers to adapt to varying weather conditions and make data-driven decisions that increase crop yield while also conserving the environment.

9.5. AI in Livestock Farming

AI's reach extends beyond crops into livestock farming. Animal tracking and recognition software allow farmers to monitor individual animal's health, diet, and reproduction cycles more effectively. Such details assist farmers in making better decisions regarding feeding, breeding, and medical treatment, leading to healthier livestock and increased farm productivity.

9.6. Implementing AI in Farming: Challenges and Future Prospects

While the possibilities of AI in agriculture are significant, embracing high tech in farming comes with its own challenges. Many small-scale farmers may find the cost of implementing AI technologies prohibitive, and there's the hurdle of technical knowledge and ability. Furthermore, aspects of data handling, privacy, and security are potential issues.

Yet, despite these challenges, the future of AI in farming offers promising prospects. The merging of AI and agriculture could result in agriculture being less damaging to the environment, more productive, and, ultimately, more capable of supporting our growing global population. With concerted effort, collaboration, and investment, AI has the potential to revolutionize sustainable farming, playing a critical role in global environmental conservation.

In the end, AI in agriculture is an evolving field with the potential to usher in the dawn of a new era in farming, where sustainability and productivity go hand in hand. It could prove to be an essential solution for developing efficient and eco-friendly farming practices while dealing with the broader issue of climate change. By integrating AI with agriculture, we are not just anticipating the future; we are reinforcing the present with sustainability at its core.

Chapter 10. Bridging Policy and Tech: The Role of AI in Environmental Governance

Understanding the correlation between technology and environmental policy is essential in this digital age. Advancements in technology, particularly artificial intelligence (AI), have given rise to a new method of approaching environmental conservation efforts.

10.1. The Historical Context

Firstly, it's important to understand why AI can be a gamechanger in the field of environmental governance. Traditional modes of monitoring and regulation have often fallen short, mainly due to the scope and complexity of environmental issues. Environmental governance is conventionally characterized by complex regulation systems, conflictual interests, and the need for multi-level coordination. More often than not, the methods employed for monitoring, anticipating risks and mitigating damages have been reactive rather than proactive, and only partially effective.

10.2. Activating AI for Environmental Surveillance

Modern tools, including AI, provide remarkable abilities in monitoring and prediction beyond what was previously conceivable. AI algorithms can process vast amounts of data to identify patterns and trends, making possible timely and proactive responses. For instance, the use of AI for real-time detection, prediction, and assessment of environmental hazards has proven effective in early alerts, minimizing potential damage, and formulating mitigation strategies.

Moreover, autonomous vehicles and drones, equipped with cameras and sensors, can gather environmental data from inhospitable regions on land, under the sea, and in the sky. Coupling these data with AI analysis, policy-makers and conservationists can gain insights and make data-driven decisions, marking a novel approach of tech-oriented environmental governance.

10.3. The Power of Predictive Modeling

Predictive modeling in AI stands as an indispensable strategic tool. It uses historical data to forecast future behavior, trends and outcomes. When it comes to environmental monitoring, it enables researchers and relevant authorities to predict the impacts of different policies and practices on the environment. Using algorithms that learn from existing data, predictive modeling offers a view of various scenarios and their potential outcomes, thus allowing us to prepare for and even prevent environmental crises.

10.4. AI-driven Policy Formulation

Technology is revolutionizing not only how we monitor and protect the environment but also how we formulate environmental policies. AI can handle the aggregation and analysis of high-volume environmental data generated from myriad sources. The ability to evaluate these vast amounts of information aids in identifying and prioritizing environmental issues. Subsequently, these insights can support the creation of comprehensive, data-driven environmental policies that cater to specific needs identified during analysis.

It is worth noting, however, that while AI is an enabler, it's only part of the answer. Governmental bodies, policy makers, and environmentalists should work together to ensure that technology and environmental policy move hand in hand. Policies should be designed to encourage the ethical use of AI in environmental governance, and the right tech solutions should be employed to support policy goals.

10.5. Carbon Tracking and Accountability

One innovative application of AI in environmental governance is carbon tracking and accountability. By employing AI to monitor, quantify and verify emissions, we have a clearer, more accurate view of the real-time global carbon footprint - at the level of individuals, industries, cities, and nations. This makes it easier to establish responsibility for emissions and better enforce existing regulations.

For example, relevant AI tools can process satellite imagery to identify concentrations of greenhouse gases released into the atmosphere. With such information readily available, holding individuals, corporations, and countries accountable for their emissions becomes a much more feasible task. It makes it easier to enforce existing regulations and draft new ones based on these insights.

10.6. Final Thoughts on AI in Environmental Governance

AI is distinguished by its potential for dynamic adaptation and continuous learning. As our understanding of environmental processes expands and improves, so too will the accuracy and usefulness of AI in managing these systems. This cycle of learning and adaptation is a powerful mechanism for ensuring that our approach to environmental governance evolves with the rapid pace of global change.

However, the integration of AI into environmental governance must observe ethical, legal, and data privacy norms. This calls for a strong legal framework to ensure that while we harness the power of AI to save our planet, we do not compromise on ethical and privacy concerns.

In conclusion, the application of AI in environmental governance paints a promising picture of proactive and efficient management of environmental concerns. By bridging the gap between technology and policy, we can look forward to more innovative ways to conserve our planet for future generations. The journey, laden with challenges and opportunities, will be transformative. The critical factor will always be a cooperative, multi-stakeholder approach, balancing the benefits of AI with observance of ethical norms, to make real, tangible progress in our fight against climate change.

Chapter 11. The Road Ahead: Future Scopes of AI in Environmental Conservation

Environmental conservation has always been a domain of complexities due to to the delicate interdependencies among various species and ecosystems, unpredictable climatic conditions, and several other myriad factors which have often perplexed even the most advanced scientific minds. Today, we are at the cusp of harnessing the power of advanced technology, specifically Artificial Intelligence (AI) and machine learning, to uncover the paradoxes of environmental conservation and climate change.

11.1. AI for Climate Predictions

The manifestations of climate change have become increasingly prominent and indeed, ominous, with the rising global temperatures, shifts in precipitation patterns, and the increase in the occurrence of extreme weather events. The unanswered question remains: "What does the future hold for climate change?"

AI holds promise in answering this query. It can leverage massive datasets consisting of historical climate data and utilize algorithms to forecast future climatic patterns. No longer are we confined to linear regression models for weather predictions; instead, we can use machine learning approaches such as neural networks that can recognize intricate patterns and dependencies in complex data.

One such AI model, developed by a team of researchers at the University of Montreal, uses AI to predict temperature and precipitation up to a year in advance with impressive accuracy. Similarly, Google's DeepMind has created machine learning algorithms that can help predict the energy output of wind farms, thereby making renewable energy a more viable option.

However, these are just the first stepping stones. The ultimate goal is to create AI models that can accurately predict how various aspects of the environment will morph in response to changes in climate over decades or even centuries.

11.2. AI for Biodiversity Conservation

Biodiversity is the nexus of a healthy ecosystem. A decrease in biodiversity due to habitat destruction, pollution, climate change, or over-exploitation of species can lead to an imbalance in the ecosystem, which can have far-reaching consequences.

AI is proving to be instrumental in monitoring biodiversity. IoT devices installed with image recognition software can help monitor wildlife health and track animal and bird movements, protecting them from illegal poaching or identifying regions where humans and wildlife frequently conflict. Technologies like eBird, a machine-learning tool that records bird species and population, can offer critical insights for conservation efforts.

The expansive scope of AI in biodiversity conservation, accommodating the monitoring of marine ecosystems through AI-powered drones and the data from satellite imaging to predict deforestation, is overwhelming but encouraging at the same time.

11.3. AI for Carbon Tracking and Management

Carbon tracking plays an essential role in the fight against climate change. Monitoring the carbon emissions from various industrial sectors helps policymakers and corporations formulate strategies to reduce their carbon footprint, ensuring conformity with international standards and regulations.

A start-up named WattTime is already utilizing AI to track carbon emissions in real-time. Google's Environmental Insights Explorer employs AI to synthesize data, providing city-level carbon footprints and renewable energy potential, enabling cities to strategize about their carbon reduction plans.

Future applications could possibly include AI-driven tracking of individual carbon footprints and providing personalized suggestions to reduce carbon emissions.

11.4. AI for Resource Management

Climate change, along with the burgeoning global population, is increasing the demand for vital resources such as water and fuel. AI's predictive powers are encouraging efficient resource management, with smart grids for electricity, water management systems, and precision agriculture as prominent examples.

In the future, we could see AI integrated even deeper into natural resource management. AI-powered systems might manage our electricity usage and water consumption in real-time, optimizing energy usage to the last bit. Precision agriculture equipped with AI could not only optimize resource utilization but also ensure food security.

In the sphere of environmental conservation and combating climate change, AI's potential is immense and largely unexplored. While harnessing AI's abilities is exciting, it also presents titanic challenges that need strategic and conscientious addressal. The implications of relying on AI, from data privacy concerns to job displacement and the specter of deep learning "black boxes", must also be cautiously navigated. Furthermore, achieving broad access to the benefits of AI and machine learning may demand investment and collaboration at an unprecedented scale.

However, surmounting these obstacles could herald a future where AI fully enables humanity to understand our planet's complexities, helping us protect and preserve the astonishing beauty and biodiversity it holds. As we delve further into the AI era, one aspect is crystal clear: to combat the most significant existential threat that our planet faces today - climate change - harnessing the power of AI is not just an opportunity; it is an imperative.